Scott Foresman

Decodable Readers 16–30
Volume 2

Editorial Offices: Glenview, Illinois • Parsippany, New Jersey
New York, New York
Sales Offices: Boston, Massachusetts • Duluth, Georgia • Glenview,
Illinois • Coppell, Texas • Sacramento, California • Mesa, Arizona

ISBN: 0-328-23360-9

Copyright © Pearson Education, Inc.

All Rights Reserved. Printed in Mexico. This publication is protected by Copyright, and permission should be obtained from the publisher prior to any prohibited reproduction, storage in a retrieval system, or transmission in any form by any means, electronic, mechanical, photocopying, recording, or otherwise. For information regarding permission(s), write to: Permissions Department, Scott Foresman, 1900 East Lake Avenue, Glenview, Illinois 60025.

1 2 3 4 5 6 7 8 9 10 VOB4 12 11 10 09 08 07 06 05

Contents

UNIT 4

Decodable Reader 16
A Party for the Geese 1

Decodable Reader 17
Whirling Girl 9

Decodable Reader 18
A Pole Bean Tent 17

Decodable Reader 19
Teller, Tailor, Seller, Sailor 25

Decodable Reader 20
A Plan Is Hatched 33

UNIT 5

Decodable Reader 21
Radio Days 41

Decodable Reader 22
All Week Long 49

Decodable Reader 23
All That Moms Do 57

Decodable Reader 24
Daughters and Moms 65

Decodable Reader 25
Selfish Shelly 73

UNIT 6

Decodable Reader 26
Black and White and Big All Over . 81

Decodable Reader 27
A Circus Life for Ben 89

Decodable Reader 28
Uncle Mycroft 97

Decodable Reader 29
The Disappearing Cat 105

Decodable Reader 30
Mike the Medic 113

Decodable Reader 16

A Party for the Geese

Written by Kenneth Freid
Illustrated by Joan Autrel

Phonics Skill			
Irregular plurals			
men	women	knives	children
leaves	geese	loaves	wolves

Each summer the Glendale Street families held a big party. On a bright June day, everybody gladly marched to Blake Pond. Men carried large boxes filled with cold drinks. Women carried big baskets and bags filled with lunch, plates, cups, forks, and knives. Children carried gear for playing games.

The pond looked peaceful. Soft breezes ruffled leaves. Ducks floated on the pond. Big, loud geese waded by the water.

"Let's play a game," Jeff Sanders suggested. "We've got plenty of people for two teams."

"We can leave lunch on the tables," Mrs. Perez said.

"I'm not playing," Mrs. Wong said, "so I will set up the tables."

The neighbors played a lively game. One team scored six runs. The other team scored seven runs.

"I'm starved!" Kelly Wong finally yelled. "It's lunchtime!"

Men, women, and children quickly went back to the tables. Then everybody saw a strange sight.

Mrs. Wong stood near the tables looking unhappy. Crackers and loaves of bread lay nearby. Seven geese honked loudly.

Everybody spoke at the same time. "What happened? What's going on? Where's lunch?"

Mrs. Wong laughed. "It looks as if wild wolves chased me. But it was really just these geese," she said.

"But let me tell you what happened. I was just taking bags of crackers and loaves of bread to the tables. Seven geese came running, honking loudly. More followed them. I tripped over geese. I waved bags to make them leave, but then a bag broke. Crackers and bread tumbled out. I got upset, but those silly geese seemed really happy!"

Everybody laughed. Mrs. Wong felt fine. They still had plenty of lunch for everybody.

"I think Mrs. Wong has been really helpful," Mr. Perez said. "Now those geese can have their own meal. They will let us enjoy our party!"

The families ate salads, chicken, potatoes, pickles, peaches, and apples. Everybody enjoyed lunch.

After eating, the neighbors watched the geese. They seemed to enjoy parties too!

Decodable Reader 17

Whirling Girl

Written by Jennifer Hills
Illustrated by Anita Morelli

Phonics Skill				
R-controlled /ėr/: ir, er, ur, ear, or				
whirling	early	word	hurled	certain
world	Turkey	dirt	earth	pearls

Shirley had talent. From the beginning her parents saw that she was going places. Early in the morning on the day after her birth, Shirley began to whirl. Mom and Dad found her spinning like a top in her crib.

"What on Earth!" exclaimed Dad.
"My word!" cried Mom.

　　Shirley was a happy baby. She became a sweet girl who liked helping out. She was happiest when spinning. She learned to use her spinning in lots of ways. She gave kids airplane rides. She hurled the shot put about a mile. Shirley could hang paintings quicker than a blink.

But Shirley was certain she could do more. How could a talent for spinning help the world?

Shirley dreamed a dream. In her dream, she became Whirling Girl! She bored a hole into the earth and saved a lost boy. She whirled rope around men who were robbing First Bank and left them in a neat bundle.

When she woke up, Shirley had a plan. She tied spades on her feet and began to spin.
"I bet I can tunnel all the way to Turkey!"
Her tunnels were huge wormholes.
"There is a lot of dirt in this yard," yelled Dad.
"What were you thinking?" asked Mom.

Shirley blurted out the story of her dream. "Shirley, you are great now!" said Dad.

"Even if you couldn't twirl, we would still think you are great," added Mom.

But Shirley felt so sad that Mom and Dad began thinking. Their thinking went round and round.

At last they had it! "Come with us, Shirley," said Mom and Dad. They drove to an ice rink. Shirley tied on ice skates.

"Meet Coach Durning," said Mom. "She will teach you to skate."

Shirley learned to soar like a bird over the ice.

Shirley learned to skate so well, she became a star. She liked her skating dress with pearls and sequins. She sparkled as she leaped and danced over the ice. But the crowd enjoyed it most when Shirley, the Whirling Girl, twirled like a top.

Decodable Reader 18

A Pole Bean Tent

Written by Neil Fairbairn
Illustrated by Lena Bartolai

Phonics Skill
Prefixes pre-, mid-, over-, out-

outdoors	outline	outside	midpoint	presoak
overcrowded	midsummer	overgrown	overhead	

Do you have a green thumb? Then try gardening for a fun way to spend time outdoors. You can get lots of fresh air—and things to eat. Think about what you can grow: peas, peppers, carrots, berries, and more.

I think beans are best. You can eat them and play with them as well. That's right, play with them. Here's how.

First, go to a garden shop and pick up a packet of pole bean seeds. Also get six thin poles, each at least six feet long.

Next, set up the planting space in the garden. On the ground, outline a circle three feet wide. Then pull weeds and turn over the dirt inside the circle with a garden fork.

Rake the ground flat. Then place six poles around the outside of the circle with their tops leaning into the midpoint. Leave a bigger space between two poles. Why? Wait and see!

Tie the pole tops with string. Now you've got a pole frame.

When days start getting hot in late spring, presoak your bean seeds. Plant them by placing six beans at the base of each pole and poking them an inch into the ground. Place dirt over them and water them daily.

In less than ten days, your bean plants will sprout.

When the bean plants are three inches high, thin them out. Take out the little ones, and leave three strong plants at each pole. The plants must not be overcrowded.

Keep sprinkling them with water, and see how fast they grow. Your plants will race up the poles.

By midsummer your bean plants will reach pole tops. The frame will be overgrown with big leaves and bright flowers. These flowers will turn into beans you can eat.

Now can you see why you left space between two poles? It's an opening for your pole bean tent!

Your bean tent is like a house with leaves and flowers growing overhead. It is a place for shade on a hot day. It is a place to play hide-and-seek or just sit inside and read.

And it has plenty of green beans to pick and eat!

Decodable Reader 19

Teller, Tailor, Seller, Sailor

Written by K. E. Theroux
Illustrated by James Connor

Phonics Skill				
Suffixes -er, -or, -ess, -ist				
actress	artist	chemist	conductor	inventor
firefighter	editor	seller	driver	sailor

"Now we'll discuss jobs," Miss Lim told her class on Friday morning after math. "We know that jobs are things that people do for a living, so first tell me what my job is."

Lola spoke quickly, "You're a teacher, Miss Lim."

"And what do teachers do?" asked Miss Lim.

"Teachers help us learn things," Jeb finally blurted out.

"Now think about more jobs that people do when they grow up," Miss Lim said, handing out paper.

"After picking one job, you'll write about that job and tell why you picked it." Little by little the room grew silent as the class started making lists of jobs.

Rose can see herself in two jobs. First, she is an artist, and she paints big red flowers and yellow suns on large white canvases. People admire her bright paintings.

Then she is an actress, and she speaks her lines in plays on stage without making a single mistake! People clap and whistle loudly for her.

Lola knows she wants a job in which she helps people.

Her uncle is a doctor, and her mom is a dentist. Lola has watched them both at work. Doctors help sick or hurt people, while dentists help people care for their teeth. Both are fine jobs, and both jobs help people. Which job should she pick?

Zan likes reading stories. Editors fix mistakes in stories before they get printed, so an editor will read lots of stories.

Zan likes listening to music. Conductors lead bands when they play, so a conductor will listen to lots of music. Which job would be better for him?

First, Jeb sees himself as a racecar driver. He sees a sleek car speeding on a racetrack, and he holds the wheel tightly as he wins the race!

Then Jeb sees himself as a teacher. He sees happy kids sitting in a classroom, and he helps them learn things—just like Miss Lim!

"Now, class," said Miss Lim. "Let's start writing. Has everybody picked a job?"

"Actress! Writer! Dentist! Inventor! Firefighter! Nurse! Conductor! Pilot! Chemist! TEACHER!"

Miss Lim smiled and held up her hands. "My, you're eager to write about your jobs! Now let's see that in your writing."

Decodable Reader 20

A Plan Is Hatched

Written by Julie Renault
Illustrated by Leslie Sidon

Phonics Skill
Syllable pattern VCCCV

complain	constant	exclaimed	hungry	inspect
impressed	instant	Mildred	monster	surprise

Constance has a big dream. Her friends think it is a very strange dream. In fact, they think her plan is a little bird-brained. That's because Constance plans to own an ostrich farm!

"An ostrich farm?" Sandra asked. "Last time we talked you were going to be an actress!"

"That's a long story," Constance replied. She then told Sandra her long ostrich tale.

One day I heard an odd noise outside. That constant, loud noise went on and on, and soon I couldn't stand it a moment longer. I went to my window to complain. Little did I know as I opened the window that my goal in life would change.

Miss Mildred, the lady next door, had a huge crate in her yard. That knocking, banging noise came from inside her crate!

"Miss Mildred," I yelled over the racket. "Why is so much noise coming from that crate?"

The banging inside Miss Mildred's crate got louder.

Miss Mildred was in a state of distress! She was so frustrated that she burst into tears.

"Constance, my dear," she replied. "I don't know how to handle this mess! This monster is a birthday gift sent by my crazy Uncle Clem, but I cannot do a single thing to control it!"

Miss Mildred slumped down sadly on her knees.

I went out to inspect Miss Mildred's "monster." When I peeked in the noisy crate, I got a complete surprise.

"It's an ostrich!" I shouted, jumping back in shock.

"Yes," Miss Mildred moaned, shaking her head. "Please, can you help me with it?"

"Maybe it's hungry. When did it last eat?" I asked Miss Mildred, edging slowly closer.

Uncle Clem had sent big food bags with this crate. We gave that ostrich a nice snack. In an instant he was quiet. He made happy little sounds as he gobbled his food.

"It was such fun to help with that big bird," Constance said. "So now I am planning a huge ranch myself, with at least a hundred ostriches!"

Sandra was impressed by Constance's grand plan. "That's exciting!" Sandra exclaimed. "It sounds like fun."

"So, Sandra," Constance added with a wink, "do you want to help me work with the ostriches?"

Decodable Reader 21

Radio Days

Written by Corey Tenon
Illustrated by Clarisse Fontana

Phonics Skill					
Syllable pattern CVVC					
audio	created	ideas	pianos	radio
stereo	video	violins	pioneers	scientists

Did you watch videos last night? Maybe you listened to music on the stereo. Most people enjoy these forms of recreation. But sixty years ago or so, you might have spent time in different ways. You likely would have listened to your family's radio.

Back in those days, radio didn't just air music or news. Families gathered around big radios in their living rooms each night. They listened happily as actors and actresses performed plays, acted out stories, and cracked jokes. Sound effects made radio plays seem real.

How did radio start? Phones were invented in 1876. Phone signals went through wires. Scientists thought air, not wires, could carry radio signals. An inventor sent radio signals through air in 1895. Soon ships at sea could make calls with radios. Radio helped save shipwreck victims.

Before long, airplane pilots and armies used radios. Everybody called radio the *wireless* since radio waves moved through air without wires.

Music first aired on radio around 1910. It wasn't pop music but classical music, including pianos, violins, and singers. Before long, radio pioneers created all kinds of programs. Radio had audio for baseball games, news, and plays. Thrilling stories and funny comic shows became well-known.

One radio program called *The War of the Worlds* aired in 1938. It is still remembered. It described how beings from outer space invaded Earth. An emcee told this frightening story as if it were real. It scared thousands. It made some listeners panic.

Radio shows delighted audiences. In the daytime, children listened to shows made for kids. At night, families laughed at comic shows. Jack Benny and Bob Hope were well-known radio comics. Later, these comics became TV stars.

During the Second World War, radio gave audiences daily war news. Then big changes took place in the 1950s. Audiences began turning to TV. Music, news, and sports still aired on radio. But radio's golden age had ended.

Decodable Reader 22

All Week Long

Written by Hilda Zadylak
Illustrated by Lily Goucher

Phonics Skill			
Homophones			
board/bored	flour/flower	here/hear	road/rode
role/roll	stair/stare	week/weak	write/right

"I'm bored," Val said to Mom. "What can I do?"

It was the middle of summer. Val tapped her fingers on the board her mom was painting.

"Look at the world around you," said Mom. "Stop and take time to observe, and you will not be bored."

"How can I begin?" asked Val.

"What do you hear?" asked Mom. "Listen hard!"

Val did not hear too much at first. At last noises came to her ears. Far away, cars whizzed along. Their motors hummed. Close by, birds sang songs and two bees buzzed. Mom's paintbrush made a whishing noise. Now here came a purring kitten. There were so many sounds to hear.

The next day, Val asked, "Now how can I observe?"

Mom knew what to ask. "What can you smell?"

Val sniffed the air. "Nothing," she said. But she found many new things to smell. One flower smelled like spice. Later Mom and Val mixed flour into cake batter. The freshly baked cake would smell sweet.

The next day as they rode in the car, Val grinned and asked, "What now?"

"What can you feel?" asked Mom.

The car seat felt hot. The glass window felt slick. Stones in the road felt sharp. Her puppy's nose was wet and cold. His fur felt soft and warm. Val liked how he felt.

Next Val tried out her taste buds. She played the role of a chef taste-testing foods. She crunched peanuts and chips. She tried pickles.

The banana she ate was sweet like cream, but a tart berry exploded in her mouth. She put jam on a hot fresh roll. That tasted best of all.

Friday was a day for seeing. Val and Aunt Lin strolled to the park. There were many things to stare at. Standing on a stair, Val watched a line of ants. Each ant held bits of leaves. Next Val and Aunt Lin sat down and watched a ballgame for an hour. It ended when a player struck out.

"Our day was fun!" Val told Mom when she returned home.

It had been a fun-filled week without even an echo of "I'm bored."

In her diary, Val would write, "The world is fu of sounds, smells, tastes, feelings, and sights."

On Saturday, Val went outside first thing. She was sure the world had many more things to teach her, and she was right!

Decodable Reader 23

All That Moms Do

Written by Elena Placido
Illustrated by Janice Fairbanks

Phonics Skill
Vowel sound in ball: a, au, aw, al

all	awful	because	lawn	squawk
tall	walnut	saw	small	always

At the end of the lawn in Jim's backyard was a tall walnut tree. Jim's dad had made a house in it, and Jim often went there to think about things. High in his treehouse, Jim felt okay. He liked hearing the wind in the leaves and seeing birds flutter from branch to branch.

One day Jim went to his treehouse because he did not want to clean his room.

"Your room is an awful mess," Mom had said. "I want you to clean it by lunchtime!"

"No! No! No!" Jim had said to himself. "It's my room, and I like it this way!"

He ran to his treehouse.

"I'll stay here for ten years," Jim said.

Jim sat in the tree and gazed at his house.

"Mom is always asking me to clean my room or make my bed," he grumbled to himself.

Just then, Jim heard a sound.

"Chirp, chirp, chirp."

Jim saw a baby bird in a nest, calling for food

A moment later a big bird landed beside the baby.

"This must be its mom," Jim decided.

The mother bird filled her baby's mouth with food.

The little bird gobbled up its dinner. Then it started squawking again.

Mother bird went off to find more food.

The big bird came and went and came and went. Jim counted thirteen trips in all. Each time she came, she gave her baby another meal.

"That mom works hard," Jim said to himself.

And suddenly he began thinking about his own mom.

"My mom works hard also. She feeds me just like that mother bird feeds her small baby."

Jim got down from the tree and returned to his house. Without a sound he went up to his room and picked up his toys. Then he cleaned up the mess on his bed and desk.

When he had finished, Jim went to find his mom. She was making lunch.

"I'm starving," Jim told her.

"What's your room like?" asked his mom.
"Go see it," said Jim.
Jim's mom came back a moment later.
"Wow, Jim! What made you clean it?" she asked.
"A little bird told me to," Jim exclaimed.

Decodable Reader 24

Daughters and Moms

Written by Matt Kooper
Illustrated by Bill Franklin

Phonics Skill				
Vowel sound in ball: augh, ough				
bought	caught	daughter	fought	ought
sought	taught	thought	brought	

Paula and her mom did not always see eye to eye. They had different ideas about clothes and meals. They fought over bedtimes and babysitters. They did not like listening to the same CDs. They seemed to disagree about many things.

Paula bought a yellow and purple shawl. Her mom said Paula did not need it and had to take it back to the mall. Paula thought that wasn't fair at all.

Mom made meat loaf with brown sauce for dinner. Her daughter ate one bite and balked. She thought it was awful and did not want to eat it. Mom told Paula to eat her dinner.

Mom said that Paula's bedtime on weekends was nine. She caught Paula watching TV at ten.

Paula thought she ought to be able to stay at home on her own when Mom went out. But Mom always brought in a baby-sitter. And that's how things went day after day. Paula and Mom almost never talked because they always seemed to disagree.

One day Mom had a cough. It didn't seem like a big deal, but the cough got worse and worse. Finally, Mom sought help from a doctor. He told her that she needed rest and ought to stay in bed resting for two weeks.

Later that day, Mom called to Paula. "We need to talk."

Mom told her daughter that she was sick and needed Paula's help. Now Paula had many jobs. First she brought her mom hot tea and oatmeal in the morning. Then she greeted Miss Fraught, the home helper, and let her into the house. Paula made her bed and washed the dishes before she walked to the bus stop.

Mom couldn't make lunches, so Paula bought her lunch in the lunchroom every day. She walked Dawg twice a day and fed him. She taught her mom some awful jokes. Mom told her some almost funny stories. They spent a lot of time together. Paula talked and Mom listened. Mom talked and Paula listened.

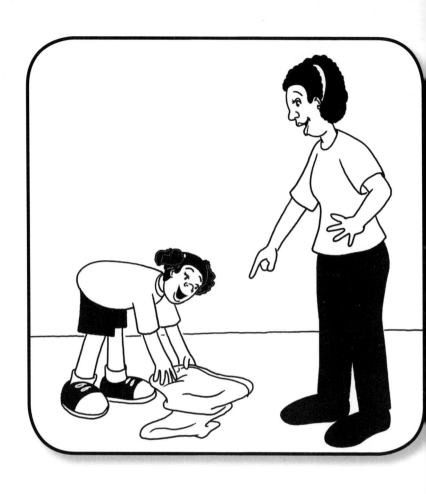

They even talked about clothes and meals and bedtimes and baby-sitters. By the time Mom was well, Paula and Mom were getting along fine. And they never disagreed again. Well, maybe they still disagreed, but only now and then. Overall, they began to see eye to eye.

Decodable Reader 25

Selfish Shelly

Written by Stephen Grantland
Illustrated by Deborah Cahill

Phonics Skill
Suffixes -y, -ish, -hood, -ment

sunny	childish	childhood	enjoyment	icy
selfish	refreshment	salty	stylish	treatment

Shelly was a good girl, but she was a little spoiled. She almost always got what she wanted. When she asked for shiny new toys, she got them. When she asked for a frisky little puppy, she got it. When she asked for stylish dresses, she got them. She thought she had a very happy childhood.

On a sunny day in June, Matt had a party for the enjoyment of all the kids in his neighborhood. When the big day came, Shelly wore her sundress made of wispy, yellowish fabric. She came late, so everyone had to wait for her before they could start playing games.

Matt had a big tray of snacks. He had crunchy nuts, buttery popcorn, chips and cheesy dip, and sticky apple treats.

"I don't like any of that stuff," Shelly said with a sniff. "I'd rather eat something more healthful." Matt was sad that he had not made Shelly happy.

Salty snacks and warm sun made the kids thirsty. They went looking for icy cold refreshment. But Shelly had taken all the water, down to the very last drop. "Well, I filled my bottle. I'm sure I will be thirsty later," she said.

Later during the party, Shelly's friends crowded around the picnic table to solve a tricky puzzle. Shelly tried to squeeze in, but no one made room for her. Di even gave her an angry glance.

Shelly sat down on the rocky ground. First she felt grumpy, but then she began to think. "I acted childish and rude," Shelly admitted to herself. "My friends did not like the bad treatment I gave them. I wish I had been kinder. If I had, right now I'd be having fun with them!"

Matt saw that she looked sad. He came to her side. "I have been selfish," Shelly told him. "I will try to think of others from now on."

Matt stuck out his hand and helped her up. "You're still our friend," he said. "We can make room at the table for you."

There was room, and Shelly did have fun. After that, she tried hard not to be so selfish.

Decodable Reader 26

Black and White and Big All Over

Written by Callie Terote
Illustrated by Lee Braden

Phonics Skill

Vowel sounds in tooth (oo, ew, ue, ui) *and* cook (oo, u)

| bamboo | bush | chew | cook | fruit |
| put | raccoon | school | Sue | zoo |

Josh dressed quickly. His long wait was almost over! Today was his class trip to City Zoo.

At nine sharp, a big school bus parked at Cook School. Josh and Brooke got on first. Soon everybody else joined them. Some children began playing wildly. Cooper jumped up on his seat. Ashley shouted loudly. Josh wasn't unruly. He just wanted to focus on zoo sights he'd see.

"Quiet, please!" Miss Rooney called. At last Josh and Brooke could hear themselves think.

"I'm excited about seeing tigers," Brooke said happily. "They're the animals I like best. Which do you like best, Josh?"

"You will find out soon," Josh replied. He smiled shyly at Brooke. Josh didn't really like keeping secrets. But talking too much about the animal might bring bad luck. He hoped he'd find it playing outside. Last time, the animal had hidden in its cool, dark cave. Josh could hardly see his furry friend.

At City Zoo, a helpful zookeeper named Sue greeted Miss Rooney's class. She began showing the excited children zoo animals. They saw lions, tigers, camels, and monkeys. Josh liked them all. At each stop, Brooke asked, "Isn't that the animal you like best, Josh?" Each time, Josh replied, "No."

At long last Sue led everybody to the animal Josh liked best. Just as Josh had hoped, it sat outdoors. It was black and white and quite big. A big black mark circled each eye.

"It looks like a large raccoon!" Martin shouted.

"It looks like a gentle grizzly bear!" Ginny yelled.

"It's not a raccoon or a bear, but it has traits of both. It's a giant panda! Which food do you think Pete Panda likes most?" Sue asked.

"Fruit?" Kevin asked. Sue shook her head.

"Meat? Noodles?" Jane asked. Sue shook her head twice.

"Leaves from a lilac bush?" Kate asked.

Josh just had to speak up. "Bamboo," he said.

"That's true," Sue nodded. "Lots of bamboo trees grow in China where pandas live. Pandas chew bamboo shoots, or tiny branches. They chew bamboo leaves as well. Aren't pandas picky? Bamboo's the only food they'll put in their mouths."

Soon everybody got back on the bus. "Now we all know which animal you like best, Josh," said Brooke. She gave Josh a high five. "Cool!"

Decodable Reader 27

A Circus Life for Ben

Written by Jenna Borman
Illustrated by Stefan Korzak

Phonics Skill
Unaccented syllables/Word parts

around	circus	family	item	seven
tickets	breakfast	afraid	juggled	moment

Long ago a family of bears lived in Berry Woods. There was Mama Bear, Papa Bear, and little Harry Benjamin Bear. It was a big name for a tiny bear. But Ben, as everybody called him, had big dreams.

Life was quiet in Berry Woods. It was way too quiet, if you asked Ben!

Ben wanted to travel around the world. He dreamed about sailing the seven seas. He would zip over bright blue water and see huge whales spout. He dreamed of climbing Earth's tallest mountain. He would plant his family's flag on it. He dreamed of exploring the darkest jungle. All wild animals would be afraid of him.

Then one day, Ben saw a poster. "A circus!" cried Ben. The Flying Bear Circus was coming to Berry Woods!

Ben liked everything about circuses. Now he dreamed about being a high-wire performer or a trapeze artist. He also dreamed about being a famous clown. A circus life was the life for Ben.

Ben thought, "I must join the circus!"
Ben packed his lucky marble and some honey. He tiptoed out of his house so Mama and Papa Bear would not wake up. He walked until he was tired. After a little rest, he reached the circus.
"We have been waiting for you," said the Circus Master.

Ben was a hit at the circus. He balanced on his head and juggled balls with his feet.

He swung gracefully on a trapeze. He let go, and the crowd gasped. At just the right moment, he grabbed his swing. Ben was safe!

He climbed into a tiny truck with a clown, and they drove around, honking the horn. Everybody cheered wildly. "Hurray for Ben!"

Ben traveled everywhere with the circus. Its train chugged over mountains and into valleys. The circus went around the world. Ben was a hot item! Tickets sold out in Paris and Rome and Calcutta.

But Ben missed Mama and Papa Bear. He felt sad. "I must go home," he cried. And that is what he did.

Mama and Papa were happy to see Ben. While they fixed breakfast, he told them all about life in the circus. Mama and Papa smiled happily and didn't seem surprised at all.

"Now will you stay home with us, Ben?" they asked.

"Yes," said Ben. "Home is the place for me!"

Decodable Reader 28

Uncle Mycroft

Written by Andy Basset
Illustrated by Sarah Shwall

Phonics Skill
Common syllables -tion, -sion, -ture

adventure	direction	furniture	mansion
potion	questions	station	vacation

Uncle Mycroft had invited Brad and his sister Ella to spend a week with him. Brad and Ella had never met Uncle Mycroft, and they had lots of questions. Why did he ask to see them now? What was he like? How did he earn his living?

"My brother Mycroft is an inventor," Dad explained. "I speak to him by phone all the time, but I haven't seen him for twenty years."

This would be their first trip without Mom and Dad. They could not get away from work so Ella and Brad traveled alone by bus.

They got a big surprise when they saw Uncle Mycroft's house. His house was an old mansion surrounded by huge trees.

Brad sighed, and Ella took a deep breath and rang the bell.

The door creaked open, but no one was in sight. All Brad and Ella saw was a room full of dusty furniture.

"I'm over here, children," said a deep voice.

Brad and Ella looked in the direction of the voice. They saw an empty armchair.

"Don't be alarmed," said the voice. "You can't see me because I'm invisible!"

So that was why no one had seen Uncle Mycroft for twenty years!

A long time ago he had invented a potion that made a person invisible. The potion worked perfectly. But Uncle Mycroft had not found a way to reverse it. He wanted Brad and Ella to buy the things he needed for more tests.

All that week Brad and Ella went shopping for Uncle Mycroft. And all that week he tested his new potion.

At last it was ready. Uncle Mycroft took a large spoonful. Nothing happened.

Suddenly Brad and Ella heard a small voice.

"It worked—well, sort of."

Brad and Ella gasped. Where was Uncle Mycroft this time?

"Look down, kids," called a cheerful voice.

They looked down and there was Uncle Mycroft. Yes, they could see him now. But he was just six inches tall.

"Not perfect, but a good start," said the tiny uncle.

At the end of the week, Brad and Ella told Uncle Mycroft that they'd visit him again whenever he needed them.

Mom and Dad met the kids at the bus station.

"Tell us all about your adventure," Dad said. "What's Uncle Mycroft like now?"

"Well, right now he's kind of like you," Ella said, "but a little shorter."

Decodable Reader 29

The Disappearing Cat

Written by J. A. Vezzetti
Illustrated by Sean Baskin

Word Structure
Multisyllabic words using word parts

carefully	disliked	hopelessness	reappeared
replacement	unbearably	unhappiest	unprepared

Henry Tucker was the unhappiest boy in Port Town. His cat Chase had disappeared six weeks ago. At first Henry wasn't worried. Chase often got the urge to wander, but he always reappeared in a few days. Henry thought that Chase would have lots of good stories to tell about his trips—if only Chase could talk!

After Chase had been gone for three days, Henry started searching for him. First he looked carefully in all the places that Chase might hide. Chase wasn't in the shed in the garden or in the maple tree by the fence. He wasn't under the porch of the red house on Vine Street.

Chase wasn't in the boxes behind the bookstore or by the food market. He wasn't in the tall grass or under the hedges around the pond.

Next Henry posted signs all over town. The signs had the word *Missing*, a picture of Chase, and a phone number. Henry waited by the phone, but no one called.

As the days went by, Henry grew discouraged. His dad took him to the animal pound. There were lots of cats there, but no Chase. Dad said, not unkindly, "Maybe you want to get another cat."

A replacement for Chase? That idea was unacceptable to Henry. Chase was much too remarkable a cat.

Henry thought about Chase all the time. He recalled that Chase often sat on Henry's desk while he worked. Chase gracefully tucked his paws and watched Henry with big green eyes. Now the desk looked impossibly empty. At night in bed Chase would curl up right next to Henry. It was a bit uncomfortable at first, but Henry got used to it. Now his bed felt unbearably lonely.

Cat ownership was often hard and messy, but all that Henry recalled now was Chase purring and rubbing on his legs. Henry had disliked it when Chase misbehaved. Now Henry wished that Chase would come back and misbehave as much as he wanted. Henry slumped lower on the steps. He was filled with fear and hopelessness.

Suddenly Chase reappeared in the yard. Unprepared for this sight, Henry didn't move. Then he grabbed and hugged the cat tightly. Chase squirmed free and licked his ruffled fur. He looked at Henry as if to say, "How about refreshments?"

Henry smiled and refilled the food and water dishes. Chase was home.

Decodable Reader 30

Mike the Medic

Written by Renee McLean
Illustrated by Kourtney Garret

Phonics Skill
Related words

act/action	breath/breathe	cloth/clothes	sign/signal
hand/handle	medic/medical	safe/safety	finally/finished

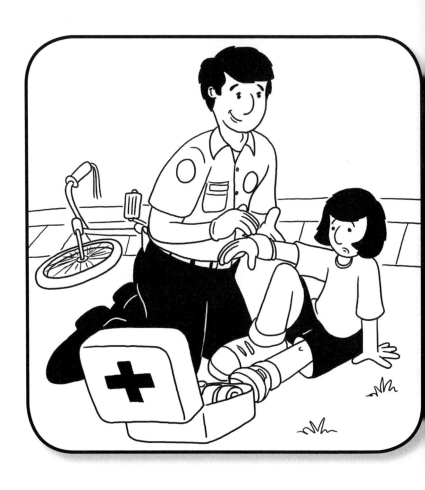

This is Mike. He is a medic. A medic helps people who have medical problems before they can get to a doctor. Mike gives first aid when people are hurt or sick. Medics help take injured or sick people to the hospital so that they can get medicine and other help needed.

Mike works for the fire department. Like many medics, he is a firefighter too. Mike sleeps at the firehouse. But Mike won't stay asleep for long. The alarm tells Mike that it is time to wake up and get to work. He gets dressed quickly and rushes to his truck. It's time for action!

The truck has lights and sirens that signal drivers to pull over to the side of the road. Bright, flashing lights and loud, wailing sirens are signs that this truck needs to get someplace fast. Cars pull over and stop to make way for this fire truck.

When the truck gets to the place where help is needed, the firefighters see smoke. A house is on fire! Mike and the other firefighters act quickly. Mike grabs the handle of his first-aid kit with one hand and blankets with his other hand. While other firefighters put the fire out, Mike checks to see if anyone is hurt.

Mike sees a family standing on the sidewalk. They look cold and frightened. Their clothes smell smoky and their faces are sooty. But everybody is safe. They had put cloth over their noses and mouths, which protected them from smoke. Mike checks them out and wraps blankets around them to keep them warm.

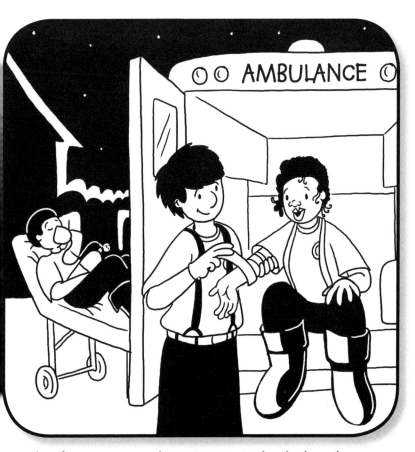

The fire is out at last. Now Mike helps the firefighters. Tim feels sick from heat and smoke. He cannot catch his breath. Mike puts a mask on his face to help him breathe clean air while he rests. Tim will see a doctor to make sure he is healthy and safe. Marla needs Mike's help too. She fell inside the house and cut her arm. Mike works hard looking after these brave safety workers.

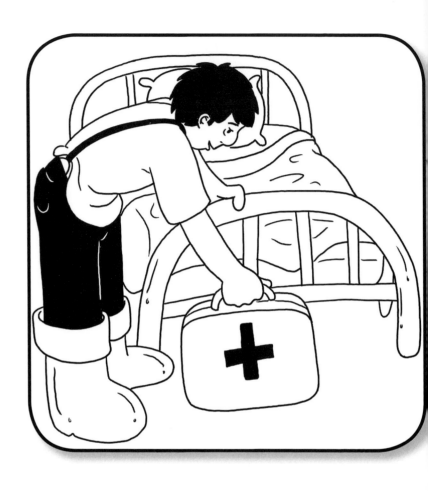

When they are finished, Mike and the other firefighters return to the station. Mike can finally get back to sleep. He is really tired now, but he is also happy that he is able to do such good work. His ability to help people every day makes Mike very proud.